THE PERNICIOUS CAUSE:

The Corrupt and Absurd Trump/Republican Agenda in America, Today!

By

Jim Green

DEDICATED TO:

Those Americans who finally *"get it"*—that we have a president who could destroy America in his pissing contest with Kim Jong, who has serious mental problems in his obsession with President Obama, who heads a political party that wants to relegate America to the 8th Century, BC--and as a result these Americans : *Have stopped voting Republican*! Amen
WEB: http://www.amazon.com/James-L.-Jim-Green/e/B001KHZIMM/ref=ntt_dp_epwbk_0

ISBN-10: 1976112893

ISBN-13: 978-1976112898

PROLOGUE

TO THE RANK AND FILE AMERICANS--WHO FOR GOD ONLY KNOWS WHY--VOTE REPUBLICAN:

Have you ever noticed that when rank and file Republicans discuss an issue…..it sounds an awful lot like every other rank and file Republican—like calling all Democrats "baby killers" [what insufferable jerks!]…..and they also sound an awful lot like FAUX [not the news!]….like they all check in to get their "marching orders" on this wacko CAUSE from the Fake News Channel….with the head scratching enigma: How do they get these "trained seals" to do that? Sigh…..

Harry Truman said it about as well as it could be said….his message to the rank and file regarding the Republican agenda [which is stabbing them in the back, rather than having their back]….and as true today as 70 years ago regarding voting Republican…

"How many times do you have to get hit on the head before you figure out whose hitting you"!

In short---the Republicans are not on your side! They don't have your back! They have the Koch brothers back—and the Republican agenda spends every waking moment pondering how to steal from you so they can give your cash to the rich—their every breath is how to screw you! Get it? Capuche?

For proof….look at their voting record….every Republican in the House…..and save for three Republicans in the Senate voted to cheat 26 million Americans out of healthcare—so they could give a gift bag of cash to people who do not need it—i.e., an obscene tax cut to the already rich for PURE GREED….and with the specific intent to screw YOU-- the rank and file!

Our pundits tell us that this segment of Americans [the rank and file who vote Republican] live in a bubble….like the schizophrenic who has withdrawn into a shell….have shut out everything except the voices in their head….except in this case the voices are limited to fake news—i.e., the right wing radio and TV nut cases, i.e., blithering idiots like Limbaugh…...

And the great enigma, today, is that the Democrats are the good guys…..the ones on the right side of history…..and calling them "liberals" as an ugly remark is absurd—espoused by people who have a profound ignorance of the English language [look up liberal, and then look up illiberal—what you are if you are not liberal….i.e., our closed/small-minded and petty]….Christ was a "liberal"--and the great enigma is why Democrats are doing such a miserable job conveying they are the good guys, etc……

And not to be confused…..Democrats are in the majority in America—Hillary got over 3 million more votes than Trump….but our problem is the millions who stay home…who are disenchanted with politics and don't see the nexus between the cause for their disenchantment, being the result of and their not voting! It was their absence from the voting booth that allowed our flawed Electoral College system to give us Trump! In addition to the possibility that our Electronic Voting was hacked, and the jury is still out on that question—see the chapter on FAIL-SAFE ELECTRONIC VOTING, herein!

Another part of this mystery is that in spite of us Democrats being in the majority—both houses of Congress, the presidency, and two-thirds of our states controlled by Republicans—it is like having a skunk at the garden party—just look at Kansas, their governor is certifiable—their education system is the worst in the nation…with one school after another closing because the governor doesn't want to pay teachers salaries! No investing in the youth in Kansas….and, an insane indifference to our future!

Which is a great segue for discussing THE CAUSE……the Republican CAUSE. The word "batshit" was invented to describe it—and it is based on flat out lies—propaganda lies and used in the same manner Goebbels used to trick the German people....

Enough adjectives.....

First is the short description of the Republican agenda—and what an incredible pile of BS it is....oops, more adjectives.....here is their snake oil: Cut taxes for the already most wealthy—and this will create jobs [the worst part of this lie], and the economy will flourish [it is PURE BS]!

First, it is indifferent to the business cycle—i.e., it ignores [lies about] downturns in the market—to even remotely work the market has to be raging constantly—which has NEVER happened! Indeed, there are few things on the planet more unstable than the market—which is not condemning the market, it is just a fact—and the market has not resulted in a UE rate below 3% since 1953! Leaving millions jobless in the interim—and turned our inner-cities into war zones!

The Republicans invented words to describe this pile of crap heaped on the American people—"Supply-Side", and "Reaganomics"—[Bush I called it "vodoo economics"]....and both times when they dumped this pile on the American people [via Reagan and Bush II] it twice trashed our economy—in 1987 and 2008—and in the latter we were within an inch of the worst depression in American history!

In short, this Republican snake oil has a shelf life of 7 years before it trashes our economy—we can't siphon America's wealth away from the consuming middle, and give it to the already most wealth [who don't need it] without sending our economy into meltdown! And anyone who doesn't understand that this is the Trump/Republican agenda to this day—is deaf, dumb and blind….and living in a bubble….!

I use a lot of exclamation points when referring to Republican policy because it is so blatantly wrong—so destructive---so absurd--it requires an exclamation point in defining, to be accurate…..!

Perhaps, it is time to give my take re the type of system we should have [which you are welcome to agree or reject—this is America, totally support dispute—and we need to end this no one is listening to anyone who disagrees with them…Amen]—

First, we have a "blended economy"….and capitalism would fold in a NY second if it weren't for the $2 plus trillion infused back into the economy from our taxes, and the $800 billion annually in Social Security Insurance claims…..so get over "socialism"….without it—we wouldn't have capitalism…..this is not being critical of capitalism….it is just a fact! I am a capitalist, always have been, and also always been a Democrat….support 100%, build a better widget—sell your company for a million bucks, and retire in Florida…..

A brief metaphor to explain….when I was a teenager I speculated on how to get rich by manufacturing something—don't remember what, now, but I was going to use Chimpanzees to put the product together—i.e., I would only be out some bananas—to increase my profits….what I didn't consider, however, is that without employment—no one could buy my product—

The phenomena is the same as Henry Ford when he raised the wage of his employees to $5 a day [exceedingly high for the time]—he reasoned that he could expand his sales by making his cars affordable to the people who were building them….

The Republican agenda today, however, does not mean well for America—it does not intend well for America—a tiny few wallow in lavish excess, while the vast majority are screwed by the Republican CAUSE….mostly Republican politicians pander to the wealthy who paid for their seat…this is the REPUBLICAN CAUSE—it has a moral value of zero, and is evident by their protagonists like Arizona's wacko, Steve Montenegro, and Sarah Palin—just to name two—and who speak in glittering generalities— saying nothing!

Over two thousand years age, Cicero nailed it "The people's good is the highest law"—and the Republican CAUSE gives their middle finger to the "people's good" which is a common sense "win-win" truism— while the Republican CAUSE is a "lose-lose"—i.e., in the long run even the 1% loses—like when their greed-driven, wacko CAUSE trashes the economy!

The most pernicious Republican lie is that "the market can provide anybody wanting a job, with a job"…as noted, this hasn't existed since 1953….and the mere existence of our "welfare system" is consummate proof!

It is pernicious because so long as we buy into this BS [and many Americans do]—we prevent creating JOBS, JOBS, JOBS which, as a result of automation, alone, has had a growing chant in every election since 1980---and our "frightened ones" [see more inside] want to build a wall to keep the Mexicans from getting our jobs—when it is robots that is the culprit—and our ONLY solution going forward in the 21st Century is via "public-sector" jobs! PERIOD! Humphrey-Hawkins had it on the nose!

Our current labor laws—which have one foot on the plantation--are to keep our laborers in their place….to be sure they show up with hat in hand when going to work, or looking for a job—and with as few rights as possible…..

Indeed, since WW II the Koch bros [a metaphor, and fact, for the 1%] have spent hundred of millions buying governors, legislators, congress—with the specific intent to eradicate employee rights and destroy our labor unions—partly for greed, but also for psychological reasons….to pander to the small-minded who need to push others down—to make others small, to make themselves feel tall...like Trump…

And in the 70 plus years since WW II—and using our "for sale" political system the 1% has cemented "at will" employment in every state [only Montana limits this destruction of employees rights to probationary employees]--i.e., and to destroy our labor unions—[half our states at present]—and the Republican goal to eliminate all labor unions!

Our economy, today, is what it is….for instance, robots/automation, alone, are resulting in fewer and fewer jobs—the further we advance into the 21st Century—and yet, our job creation model, today, is still lodged in the 18th Century—with our evolving sabotaged because it is propagandized to be "communism, or socialism, or God forbid "liberal"—i.e., our economy is being suffocated by idiocy!

It has given the book "What's The Matter With Kansas?"—a whole new twist…..the premise in "Kansas" asks why on Earth would poor people vote against their own economic interests [why on Earth would they vote Republican?]—

The twist, is that many in the 1%'s want to relegate American employees to A POOL OF SLAVES: To Be Used And Discarded "at will" [they have spent a fortune since WW II, buying politicians to cement "at will" employment in every state—only Montana limits to probationary employees—and to destroy labor unions in America]—but with "automation", alone, eroding our consumer base—the twist is that clinging to these 18th Century notions eats into corporate profits!

Unemployment is a No One Wins –the jobless lose, civility loses [Ferguson, et al], and the Market loses, to wit:

THE LAW OF DIMINISHED INCOME TO THE MARKET FROM UNEMPLOYMENT [hereafter D/UE LAW]

3% is the zero-sum threshold above which unemployment triggers inflation by diminishing labor training and skills, under-utilizing capital resources, reducing the rate of productivity advance, increasing unit labor costs, reducing the general supply of goods and services--and the loss in income to the Market is compounded exponentially with each percentage point of increase in unemployment, above 3%.

In short, the Koch brothers are shooting themselves in the foot by clinging to these 18th Century notions about abolishing Job Security—i.e., abolishing "employee rights" in America—

In our 21st Century economy—it cuts into corporate profits—and thus it can now be asked—as asked in "Kansas"—Why are the Koch brothers acting against their own economic interests?

For clarity….I am a capitalist….I support, 100%--build a better widget, sell your company for a million bucks, and retire in south Florida—and it is our current job creation methodology that puts this in jeopardy….

As noted…if you question capitalism, today, you don't become a heretic, per se---but rather a communist…..which is patently absurd….and it is this type of sabotage that prevents our applying solutions that actually work in our 21st Century economy…..

And the most glaring flaw in our current methodology is counting on the market to solve our unemployment problem…with the belief that "the market can provide anybody wanting a job, with a job" which has singularly driven our job creation policy since WW II—When in fact, only once since WW II has this resulted in an unemployment rate below 3%--IN 1953—leaving millions jobless in its wake, and turning our inner-cities into war zones, with an epidemic of gun violence!

Unemployment has oft severe social consequences—but currently our policy makers don't have a clue how to solve……because they are beholden to the above fraudulent propaganda/belief that the market can provide everybody with a job!

To briefly illustrate, In the mid-1970's the world economy underwent a major paradigm shift—and while economists disagree over why—all agree with Dr.

William F. Mitchell that "High and persistent unemployment has pervaded almost every OECD country since the mid-1970's" [with double digit unemployment common in the Eurozone to this day, and youth unemployment north of 25% in Greece and Spain].

As a result of high unemployment in the 1970's, however, America swung into action--and in 1978 Congress passed, and President Carter signed into law a "legal authorization" to henceforth limit America's unemployment rate to "3%", permanently [15 USC § 3101—i.e., at no time should our unemployment in America exceed 3%, as provided by law].

With a ton of cash, however, the 1% has inexplicably prevented this law from ever being implemented. Full employment is a pro-market solution, and given "automation", alone, this law is indispensable to the effective functioning of our 21st Century economy.

The purpose of this book is to urge the enforcement of this concept [currently HR 1000, in Committee].

Communism, like liberal are used as derisive words in Republican lexicon to sabotage progress…. change….which prevents urgently needed changes--- Our method for solving problems is sabotaged….

If you speak ill of the problems capitalism is incapable of solving—you are automatically labeled a communist, or liberal….

The "social issues" which have so enslaved many who vote Republican…is based on their vision of the kind of world they would like to see….like a world without gays, or women who have sex---people who are not comfortable in their own skin, and all believe "sex is a sin"—and since the world is moving in another direction they are convinced that the world is going to Hell in a hand basket….[Trump and Trump's voters]….

And to change gears slightly, when we have tried "privatization" to solve our social problems—it has been a disaster:

For instance, essential programs have been cut—such as the elimination of text books from the Job Corps education program—to increase profits, and cronyism has run rampant—

And in our "for profit" healthcare system, billions of dollars are siphoned away from the premiums we send in—and do not go to the healthcare of ANYONE—but rather is used to pay for lobbyists, to make the CEO's filthy rich—and spent on propaganda ads to keep it that way!

Further, it attracts a few who see healthcare as a means to get rich, rather than cure the ill….

Finally, the "Republican Party"—many who vote Republican, today, doesn't exist anymore! During the Eisenhower years it did not even occur to Eisenhower to attack Social Security Insurance—[unlike many insufferable Republican jerks like Paul Ryan, et al] its success as a social program had absolute clarity in America in that era…..Indeed, Eisenhower expanded Social Security coverage to include the disabled, as well as the elderly—who are unable to work!

It is like Trump putting DACA on the chopping block—it is not only stupid, it is just plain evil—and while in line with Trump's certifiable obsession/fear [and racism] to obliterate everything "Obama"—i.e. Trump is the quintessential Republican today—an INSUFFERABLE JERK who bears no resemblence to the Eisenhower Republican!

A few closing comments in the Prologue—As Oscar Wilde averred "The only truly worthless opinion is an unbiased one"—so bias, agreed—but always in the interest in getting at the larger goal—the truth….

Incidentally, I published my first book on my 78th birthday [I am currently 83—so just hang out for the nuggets when I wander…]—and not that I write that fast, or well—the materials were all there for the better part of the past 30 years, give or take, gathering dust—it was just a matter of pulling them together in some order—also, don't believe any book should be over 60 pages, plus/minus— i.e., can be read in the crapper-- two hours, max--lol—but it seems best summed up by a very astute observer [wish I could recall their name to give credit]: Persons who write do so because they have no choice [it is a compulsion, an addiction..]—they become an "author", however, when people start reading what they have written….

Finally, a note to the reader—the papers and letters are not in sequence, and apologize for redundancy [please look for the nuggets…Thx--lol]—also, if you are a "typo-wonk"—are more concerned with sentence structure, etc., than content—you probably won't like my writing—and you will find a wayward capital letter, here and there, and appearing out of place and used for emphasis—or a missing page…Hey, I'm an Indie….I chalk most up to editorial license and tongue-in-cheek, self-effacing humor—so apologies, here—[I seriously support: Take what you do seriously, but never yourself….]….

Just look for content, please….THX

CHAPTER ONE

Editor: NY TIMES

We have an opioid crisis in America, and the following is a proposed solution:

We do an enormous disservice to our youth by not providing an opportunity to work and be a productive member of society—a given in primitive societies, but lost in the Age of Industrialization--and if only one drug-related death is prevented by our stepping up to the plate on behalf of our youth…..the cost will be well worth it!

To expand on what is being proposed: First, in creating jobs, it is essential that our mind-set is based on the truism that we have far more work that needs to be done in America, than persons to fill these jobs. The notion of "make work" jobs is a relic notion of the past, that doesn't work in our 21st Century market economy.

A few Americans are aware…unfortunately too few…that we have the "legal authorization" on the books in America, as I write, to limit our youth unemployment to 4% [Pubic Law 15 USC § 3101]—i.e., at no time should our youth unemployment exceed 4%--[3% if over age 21]—and anyone wanting to work should be able to find a job.

And thus, fortunately in America we have the "legal authorization" to fix this problem. Unfortunately, however, Congress has yet to implement this law, which they passed--and not inconsequential, we stood on one foot and then the other and let Flint and the Rust Belt rot into decay—when we had the legal authority to prevent--creating a resentment that lingers to this day—and with unconscionable consequences!

To fund, proposed here is pro-market, deficit-neutral: **THE NEIGHBOR-TO-NEIGHBOR JOB CREATION ACT [Amazon--hereafter NTN]: A federally mandated Social Insurance, owned by our employed, to provide a fund to hire/train our unemployed.**

With the priority to hire our youth who want to work, but can't find a job. And as noted, if this prevents even one drug-related death it will be well worth the modest cost.

In closing, there are an abundance of jobs that go unfilled—that can be filled via "grant-in-aid" type of job proposals—from our school districts, libraries, etc.

Jim Green, candidate for the City Counsel.....

CHAPTER TWO

President Trump/Council of Economic Advisers:

It is time to end the war of words that divides Democrats and Republicans—and on healthcare, alone, henceforth put the American people first and deal honestly about our economy:

Capitalism is ideal in producing and selling corn flakes and cars—It doesn't work in solving "social problems" such as unemployment and our healthcare....

And when we have tried "privatization" to solve our social problems—it has been a disaster:

For example, essential programs have been cut—such as the elimination of text books from the JOB CORPS EDUCATION PROGRAM—TO INCREASE PROFITS, and cronyism has run rampant—

And in our "for profit" healthcare system, billions of dollars are siphoned away from the premiums we send in—and do not go to the healthcare of ANYONE—but rather is used to buy elections, pay for lobbyists, to

make the CEO's filthy rich—and spent on propaganda ads to keep it that way!

Additionally, President Obama had a weapon in 2009, not available to FDR: Were it not for the $800 billion in Social Security Insurance moneys percolating up through our economy annually in 2008—we would not be talking about having narrowly averted another Great Depression—We would have been buried in one!

The truth is, we have a blended economic system—and the two components are, in fact, indispensable to each other:

Social Insurance is a vital ingredient in building a vibrant and decent society—And, invent a better widget, sell the company for a million bucks, and retire in Florida [capitalism]—is as well a vital ingredient in building a vibrant and decent society.

So why do we have this war of words pitting the two against each other—rather than educating the American people regarding the indispensable symbiotic relationship they have to each other?

Were it not for the $2 trillion + Washington infuses back into the economy annually—capitalism would fold in a NY Second!

Regarding "unemployment" [hereafter UE]—it is essential that we evolve, and given "robots", alone, in our 21st Century economy we need to look upon UE the same as we look upon Cancer, or Polio--a ubiquious disease—a menace to society, in need of eradication via Public Law 15 USC § 3101—[currently HR 1000] which will restrict our UE to 3%, permanently—and is INDISPENSABLE to the EFFECTIVE functioning of our 21st Century market economy!

Jim Green, Democrat candidate for Congress, 2000

Thank you for contacting the White House

CHAPTER THREE

President Trump:

The number one issue by the electorate in this election was "JOBS, JOBS, JOBS, and both Hillary and Trump promised they would create "millions of jobs", if elected—but the critical question asked of neither by our media, is: "What is your method for creating these jobs"?

It is critical because Americans believe we are "moving in the wrong direction" because our methods of Job Creation since WW II DON'T WORK! [ideology has nothing to do with it—the solution lies in "what is effective?"].....

Since WW II, our method of Job Creation has been based on a fraud—that "the market can provide anybody wanting a job, with a job".....when even a cursory review of the data reveals that this method of Job Creation has not resulted in an unemployment rate below 3% since 1953! Leaving millions jobless in its wake, created inner-cities with an epidemic of gun violence, and resulted in the rot in Flint, and the Rust Belt!

Further, in 1980, the Republicans doubled down on this fraud with Supply-Side—"Voodoo Economics"—and pitched it to the American people via the snake oil: Cut

taxes for the 1% , they will build factories all across our fair land with the windfall of cash [they promise], jobs will rain down like moonbeams, and everyone will have a job in the factory---Yes folks, it is a fairy tale—and pure BS….

In addition to blowing the extra cash on themselves—rather than creating jobs—this "Voodoo" has resulted in excessive unemployment over 70% of the time since 1980 [twice the % of preceding years]—and when the Democrats failed to fix unemployment with the "legal authorization" in Humphrey-Hawkins--currently HR 1000, in Committee—in 2009 [when we could]—a retaliatory electorate filled the House with lunatics in the 2010 election—and Washington has been in paralysis ever since!

The over-arching point, here, is akin to the maxim: Doing something ineffective, or wrong, over and over, and expecting a different result is [fill in the blank]—our Job Creation since WW II—DOESN'T WORK---THE DATA IS THE PROOF! [and President Trump will fail if he returns to Supply Side, as suggested—given "automation", alone, going forward--our ONLY path to fix unemployment in the 21st Century is Pro-Market, deficit-neutral HR 1000, and/or THE NEIGHBOR-TO-NEIGHBOR JOB CREATION ACT (hereafter NTN) Amazon/Kindle].

Jim Green, Democrat opponent to Lamar Smith, Congress, 2000

CHAPTER FOUR

POSTINGS ON FACEBOOK

President-elect Trump has promised "millions of jobs" if elected….his ONLY means to accomplish this in our 21st Century market economy, is via:

THE NEIGHBOR-TO-NEIGHBOR JOB CREATION ACT [hereafter NTN, Amazon/Kindle]:

A Pro-Market, deficit-neutral, federally mandated Social Insurance, owned by our employed, to provide a fund to hire/train our unemployed. For a modest 4% of salary policy cost, triggered by the "legal authorization" in Public Law 15 USC § 3101 [currently HR 1000, in Committee], Trump will create more "private-sector" jobs IN 6 MONTHS, than the failed Republican snake oil to cut taxes for the 1% and pray they will create jobs--rather than spend the windfall of cash on themselves as they did before—IN 6 YEARS!

The Carrier jobs deal is to perpetuate a lie, a fraud on the American people—and the reference is not to the taxpayer's corporate welfare to make it work, but rather the lie that "the market can provide anybody wanting a job, with a job"—the fairy tale job creation policy that has not resulted in an unemployment rate below 3% in America since 1953—has turned our inner-cities into war zones, with an epidemic of gun violence! Further 800 jobs is a joke, when we need to

create 200,000 jobs a month in America, just to keep up with our birthrate….in any event, IT IS IMPOSSIBLE TO BE A CHRISTIAN, AND VOTE REPUBLCAN, Amazon/Kindle

For clarity…..Defining oneself as a Christian, is to follow his teachings—BY DEFINITION—why else would anyone call themselves a Christian? And the Republican agenda, today, is a repudiation of EVERYTHING Christ stood for, and spoke out against—thus the book—

CHAPTER FIVE

Fareed Zakaria, GPS, et al….

When we start with the mind-set that "We have far more work that needs to be done in America, than we have persons to fill these jobs"—we come out with a far different result in solving our unemployment crisis—and whether the powers that be want to admit it, or not—WE HAVE AN UNEMPLOYMENT CRISIS IN AMERICA [and throughout the OECD]!

It is the reason over 70% of Americans believe "We are moving in the wrong direction!"….

Also, by approaching this crisis with the above mind-set it cultivates the imagination to focus on real solutions…..to think of real work that needs to be done, that is currently ignored……

And at present, we are stuck with the totally fraudulent mind-set that "our unemployed are lazy and don't want to work"…..which has PREVENTED us from finding a solution for OUR UNEMPLOYMENT CRISIS!

Since WW II Americans have been stuck with the BS that "the market can provide anybody wanting a job, with a job"—and this fraud, perpetrated on the American people, has not resulted in a UE rate below 3% since 1953! Leaving millions jobless in the interim—and created an epidemic of gun violence!

The bottom line is that unemployment is a NO ONE WINS—the jobless lose, civility loses [Ferguson, etc.,], and THE MARKET loses, to wit:

OUR SLUGGISH ECONOMY RESULTNG FROM THE LAW OF DIMINISHED INCOME TO THE MARKET FROM UNEMPLOYMENT [hereafter D/UE LAW]

Short Definition:

> 3% is the zero-sum threshold above which unemployment starts substantially undermining the Market--and the loss in income to the Market is compounded exponentially with each percentage point of increase in unemployment, above 3%.

We have several deficit-neutral/Pro-Market paths to Full Employment—and all being sabotaged by BLIND GREED.....for one, HR 1000 [in Committee]—proposed, here, is: THE NEIGHBOR-TO-NEIGHBOR JOB CREATION ACT [hereafter NTN] Amazon—a federally mandated, Social Insurance, owned by our employed to provide a fund to hire/train our unemployed. Jobs beget jobs, and for a modest 4% of salary policy cost will create more "private-sector jobs" in 6 months, than HR 2847, in 6 years!

Specifically, every local jurisdiction in America would be eligible for a Grant-In-Aid from the Labor Department—with this Act triggered by the "legal authorization" in Federal Law 15 USC § 3101—anytime our UE rate rises above 3%.

Jim Green, Democrat opponent to Lamar Smith, Congress, 2000

PS Apologize for CAPS—your software does not permit emphasis

CHAPTER SIX

President Obama/Council of Economic Advisers:

The Democrats lost the election because they DIDN'T FIX UNEMPLOYMENT! It is the reason over 70% of Americans believe "We are moving in the wrong direction"!

But the reason is not from lack of interest, or dedication, on the part of us Democrats—[or even prevented by an obstructionist Republican Congress]---RATHER, it is because we Democrats drank the Kool Aid that "The market can provide anybody wanting a job, with a job"…..and we passed The HIRE Act--HR 2847—in 2009 as our Job Creation law—but it is an "out to lunch" law—because it is a "stop-gap" law waiting for the market to solve the problem [as opposed to "renewal funding"]—

And we Democrats then stood on one foot and then the other waiting on the Market to do something IT IS IMPOSSIBLE FOR THE MARKET TO DO [the issue isn't ideological—it regards something THAT DOESN'T WORK]!

But we Democrats went on BELIEVING in spite of the data that this, our method of Job Creation since WW II--has NOT resulted in a jobless rate below 3% since 1953! Leaving millions jobless in its wake, created our

inner-cities with 60% minority unemployment, drug economies, and an epidemic of gun violence!

But wishing hope against hope that something will work--THAT DOESN'T WORK—is not limited to us Democrats—and is akin to those folk in the Rust Belt who believe Trump's promise that he will create "millions of jobs"………..

UNLESS, Trump can wrap his brain around the fact that Hunphrey-Hawkins [currently HR 1000] is a PRO-MARKET solution…and given "automation", alone, is INDISPENSABLE to the EFFECTIVE functioning of our 21st Century market economy! AND, that Trump recognizes that unemployment adversely impacts the "bottom line"—i.e., that people do not buy what we manufacture, when they are jobless [which inexplicably is not cited by Democrats that we need to change the dialogue], to wit:

OUR SLUGGISH ECONOMY RESULTNG FROM THE LAW OF DIMINISHED INCOME TO THE MARKET FROM UNEMPLOYMENT [hereafter D/UE LAW]

Short Definition:

> 3% is the zero-sum threshold above which unemployment starts substantially undermining the Market--and the loss in income to the Market is compounded exponentially with each percentage point of increase in unemployment, above 3%..

The Solution: HR 1000 [in Committee], THE NEIGHBOR-TO-NEIGHBOR JOB CREATION ACT [NTN]Amazon: a Pro-Market, deficit-neutral federally mandated Social Insurance, owned by our employed— to provide a fund to hire-train our unemployed. Jobs beget jobs, and this will create more "private-sector" jobs in 6 mos, than HR 2847, in six years!

Jim Green, Democrat candidate for Congress, 2000

Thank you for contacting the White House!

CHAPTER SEVEN

THE HISTORY OF HOW WE GOT WHERE WE ARE
[WW II to Present]

Following WW II, President Truman signed into law the [FULL] EMPLOYMENT ACT of 1946, to provide employment for our returning troops.

Ironically, half-way around the world, Australia codified into their law an almost identical Bill, and for the same reason—

Difference is—Australia actually put their law into effect, and over the next 30 years it was intrinsic to employment policy in Australia that "anybody wanting to work should be able to find a job"—and save for a brief recession in 1961/62 their unemployment was 2%, or less. This period is still referred to as their "Golden Age", in Australia.

Unforeseen by either country, however, in the mid-1970's the world economy underwent a major paradigm shift as a result of the colliding forces of automation, globalization, technology, etc., reaching a critical mass—in brief, an adjustment towards modernity—From a perverse perspective, we became victims of our success....

The instability caused by this transition, however, resulted in a malaise, and ushered in the ill-winds of greed-driven neo-liberalism with its indifference to unemployment, and the likes of Thatcher and Reagan—and the menace of this greed-driven agenda was exploded by Bush II, resulting in obscene disparities in wealth that persists, and is the cause of much friction between right and left, to this day.

It also ushered in high and pervasive unemployment throughout our market-driven economies, the OECD—with 6% unemployment in Australia now the norm, and double-digit unemployment common throughout the Eurozone, to this day.

As a result of the "malaise", however, the U.S. took an aggressive, pro-active role in addressing the, above, economic shift—and in 1978 President Carter signed into law one of the most important laws in the 20th Century--an expansion of President Truman's full employment, i.e., Pro-Market 15 USC § 3101--which provides a "<u>legal authorization</u>" to create a "reservoir of public employees" [indispensable to the effective functioning of a 21st Century market economy]--at any time our unemployment in America exceeds "3%"—

But in spite of 3% unemployment being the threshold point above which unemployment starts substantially undermining the Market—this <u>legal authorization</u> has never been implemented--

And in spite of deficit-neutral HR 1000, or The Neighbor-To-Neighbor Job Creation Act—A federally mandated Social Insurance, owned by our employed, to provide a fund to hire/train our unemployed—[more on the critical need to apply this job creation methodology in a 21st Century market economy, ahead]….

Ref: FULL EMPLOYMENT IS A PRO-MARKET CONCEPT, Amazon/Kindle

Jim Green, Democrat opponent to Lamar Smith, Congress, 2000

CHAPTER EIGHT

THE HISTORY OF HOW WE GOT WHERE WE ARE

[Mid-1970's to Present]

In the mid-1970's, the colliding forces of automation, technology, globalization, etc., reached a critical mass—resulting in a Market no longer capable of producing the jobs necessary to its viability, and causing ubiquitous unemployment in all of the OECD countries—and leaving their leaders conflicted, ever since, regarding the displaced employee. Eurozone unemployment is still in double digits, and Greece and Spain both in excess of 20%, plus. High unemployment was also a major factor in Arab Spring.

In the U.S., we took a pro-active role in addressing this economic shift—and in 1978 President Carter signed into law 15 USC § 3101--which "authorizes" the creation of a "reservoir of public employment" at any time our unemployment in America exceeds "3%".

In 1979, however, and in a panic over Humphrey-Hawkins—our ultra-conservative foundations, and desperate to promote the Supply-Side fraud, embraced a flawed paper by an obscure MIT student, David L. Birch "The Job Generation Process"; and [with lots of cash] gave his paper biblical importance, and every president since has cited his finding as gospel.

Birch's paper concluded that "small businesses" were the greatest generator of new jobs—problem is, for the purposes of policy-making—it is BS. In a study at Harvard University in 2010, "The Myth of Small Business Job Creation" The research shows "no systematic relationship between firm size and growth." And that small businesses can actually detract from job growth.

In spite of this, however, Washington struggles, still, to make this antiquated notion, work--that it is only the market that can create jobs—and the result has been a disaster, politically as well as otherwise!

It would be impossible to still have 7.8% unemployment—if we were on the right path—and among other problems with this concept--if the market fails, the unemployed are out of luck.

Further, unemployment is a "social" problem we are seeking to address with a highly unstable, incompatible entity: The Market

What apparently isn't clear going forward is that an expanding and contracting public workforce is an indispensable component to the effective functioning of a modern market economy—

The market thrives when we have a robust, employed, consuming workforce—and overlooked is that HR 1000 [currently in Committee], and the proposed "Neighbor-To-Neighbor Job Creation Act" www.Inclusivism.org [both authorized under Humphrey-Hawkins], are deficit-neutral--Pro-Market "win-win" solutions:

The American people win, and capitalism wins—

Jim Green, Democrat candidate for Congress, 2000

CHAPTER NINE

Friends: In the event you have gotten this far—according to the Federal Election Commission, I am a candidate for president in the 2016 election—and rest assured I am not delusional, or like Trump…on an ego trip…..I filed solely to deliver a message—you are reading it—and to urge passage of the above legislation….

To Whom It May Concern—in Washingon:

OUR CHOICES ARE: Adapt and change in a world that is changing, whether we like it or not, OR be forced to create a Police State to hold our anachronistic policies, practices and laws in place—

And in America, today, we have chosen the latter…..and as only one pernicious example, of thousands—Ferguson is the result….

In a comedic, but religious context we hear of persons asking God for a sign—anything—which will warn us that we are on the wrong path, and need to change direction…..and our Police State choice, above, is our sign…..few are listening….

To illustrate a critical area in which we need to adapt and change in a 21st Century economy: We have far more work that needs to be done in America, than we have persons to fill these jobs—And 86% of Americans believe that "Anybody wanting to work should be able to find a job"---So, why on earth in a democracy, do we have 9 million jobless Americans—[per the 11/14 DOL Jobs report]?

The answer is because our method of job creation in America is based on a Fairy Tale! Specifically, our current one and only job creation methodology in America, is based on the myth/sacred cow:

"The market can provide anybody wanting a job, with a job"—

Problem is—it is pure BS—and only once since WW II has this methodology resulted in an unemployment rate below 3%--in 1953 [i.e., which translates into 5 million left jobless]--because the market cannot create enough jobs—in short, the jobs for this 5 million jobless--don't exist!

The right-wing propaganda mills trick our fools into believing that the market has created this 5 million jobs, but because those on welfare are "lazy and don't want to work" this 5 million jobs go unfilled—but that is pure balderdash!

The vast majority of persons on welfare, are there because the market cannot create enough jobs, i.e., the market lacks the viability to create these jobs—the jobs simply do not exist!

And as further proof, according to the CBO, on our current path it will be 2017 before America returns to even an anemic 5.5% unemployment rate [following the Great Recession] and if the market fails in the interim—the jobless are out of luck!

Further, this travesty is compounded because the Republicans cling to devious and discredited Supply Side Economics [to this day] as a solution, to wit:

Siphon America's wealth away from the consuming middle—give this windfall of cash to the Koch Bros [a metaphor for the 1%, hereafter "KB"]—they will build factories all across our fair land—everyone will have a job in the corporation—and we will all live happily ever after—Yes, folks it is a fairy tale!

And what we learned from this dark cloud over America is what Bush I called it long ago—before America was subjected to this devious scam—i.e., Supply-Side is "VooDoo Economics"!

So why have we allowed ourselves to be deceived by this Republican scam—[handcrafted by a plutocracy/oligarchy that still has one foot on the plantation]? But I don't want to giveaway the surprise ending—and some of my response isn't printable....! Further, and to say it up front....I am a capitalist—I support 100%: Build a better widget, sell it for a million bucks, and retire in South Florida....it is the Republican agenda, today, that is anti-market...more on this throughout.....

When President Carter handed the reigns over to Reagan in 1981—he left America with a very modest $60 billion deficit—as a direct result of Supply-Side, however, when Republicans held the White House [Clinton actually cut the deficit]—this $60 billion ballooned to a staggering $10 trillion by 2008—and it has cost Americans an additional $7+trillion to clean up this Republican mess—

Ask any economist: Our only way out of a meltdown is to buy our way out! [it was the lesson learned from the Great Depression].

And anyone who thinks McCain, had he been elected, would not have addressed this with a Stimulus, the same as President Obama in 2009—is stuffed between the ears with rice pudding……

Further, we learned that we cannot siphon America's wealth away from the consuming middle, and give it to the "KB"—without sending our economy into meltdown—as occurred in 1987 and 2008—in short, the Supply-Side scam has a shelf-life of about 7 years before the economy collapses—and as noted, costing the taxpayers trillions to put a floor under a disappearing economy!

And another fallout/direct result from this dark chapter is the disparity in wealth it has created in America—AKA the "wealth gap"--and currently the "richest 1 percent in the United States now own more wealth than the bottom 90 percent"—the second highest in our history, the first was just before the Great Depression.

A couple of other factors that played into the above scenario—when every waking moment in capitalism is spent pondering how to eliminate as many of us humans, as possible, from the workplace—to increase "profits"—why, on Earth, would we look to the market to solve our unemployment crisis in America?

As well, few things on earth are more unstable than the market….we can count on one hand the number of corporations in America that were around in 1900….with tens of thousands long since disappeared; and given "automation", alone, the market will produce fewer and fewer jobs the further we advance into the 21st Century.

Further, unemployment is a "social" problem—we, as the larger society have the responsibility to solve—i.e., it is unrealistic to expect the market to solve this problem—the market is in the "for profit" business, not the social work business—and the former would not long be in business--if they were…for example, we should never condemn the CEO for closing a plant when they are losing money—but we should be outraged by a government that doesn't have a clue re the displaced employees…..

Also, unemployment is a <u>no one wins</u> …..the jobless lose, and market loses, to wit:

3% is the zero-sum threshold above which unemployment triggers inflation by diminishing labor training and skills, under-utilizing capital resources, reducing the rate of productivity advance, increasing unit labor costs, and reducing the general supply of goods and services--and the loss in income to the Market is compounded exponentially with each percentage point of increase in unemployment, above 3%.

Short Definition:

3% is the zero-sum threshold above which unemployment starts substantially undermining the Market--and the loss in income to the Market is compounded exponentially with each percentage point of increase in unemployment, above 3%.

In sum, our job creation should be based on: Fix unemployment, and this will fix the market [HR 1000], rather than [our current mind-set] Fix the market, and this in turn fix unemployment [HR 2847] – with a result that has been a disaster—as we inch along in our job recovery, see data above, and when we didn't Fix Unemployment a retaliatory electorate ushered in a House filled with lunatics in the 2010 election, and then doubled down in 2014!

Look around—all signs in our economy are up—and yet over two-thirds of our rank and file believe "we are moving in the wrong direction"—their perception is that our economy is in the tank—that we are in an economic malaise—a condition that would disappear overnight if we did, in fact, Fix Unemployment!

Best guess is that Congress passed, and President Obama signed into law HR 2847 [the HIRE Act], in 2009—which is based on fix the market, and this will fix unemployment [180 degrees off course]—but they did this because of the pervasive [but false] belief that "The market can provide anybody wanting a job, with a job"—it is pure BS……it doesn't work! Had we insisted on putting a lawnmower engine in the rocket to get us to the Moon….we would never have gotten there…[same difference]….and all of the empirical evidence is proof HR 2847 didn't create anywhere near the jobs needed…

Jim Green, Democrat opponent to Lamar Smith, Congress, 2000

CHAPTER TEN

HOPPER-READY: THE NEIGHBOR-TO-NEIGHBOR JOB CREATION ACT

[1] PROPOSED LEGISLATION:

THE NEIGHBOR-TO-NEIGHBOR JOB CREATION ACT

A Pro-Market, deficit-neutral, federally mandated, Social Insurance, owned by our employed, to provide a fund to hire/train our unemployed.

SECTION 1. SHORT TITLE.

> **This Act shall be cited as The Neighbor-To-Neighbor Job Creation Act [To establish employment/training opportunities for the unemployed in compliance with the "Legal Authorization" in Public Law 15 USC § 3101, for the creation of a "reservoir of public employees", anytime our unemployment rate exceeds "3%", with an emphasis on training for market needs, including a training stipend, where there is a shortage of trained workers--hereafter NTN].**

SEC. 2. DEFINITIONS.

In this Act the following definitions apply:

(1) SECRETARY- The term `Secretary' means the Secretary of Labor.

(2) STATE- The term `State' has the meaning given such term in section 102(2) of the Housing and Community Development Act (42 U.S.C. 5302(2)).

(3) TRUST FUND- The term `Trust Fund' refers to the Department of Labor Full Employment Trust Fund.

(4) UNIT OF GENERAL LOCAL GOVERNMENT- The term `unit of general local government' has the meaning given such term in section 102(1) of the Housing and Community Development Act (42 U.S.C. 5302(1)).

(5) URBAN COUNTY- The term `urban county' has the meaning given such term in section 102(6) of the Housing and Community Development Act (42 U.S.C. 5302(6)).

(6) WEB SITE- The Secretary shall establish an Internet Web site to serve as an information clearinghouse for job training and employment opportunities funded by the Trust Fund.

SEC. 3. EMPLOYMENT OPPORTUNITY GRANTS TO STATES, LOCAL GOVERNMENT.

(a) Use of Funds-A recipient of a grant under this section shall use the grant primarily for infrastructure repair, including, but not limited to:

(A) The painting and repair of schools, community centers, and libraries.
(B) The restoration and revitalization of abandoned and vacant properties to alleviate blight in distressed and foreclosure-affected areas of a unit of general local government.
(C) The augmentation of staffing in Head Start, child care, and other early childhood education programs to promote school readiness and early literacy.
(D) The renovation and enhancement of maintenance of parks, playgrounds, and other public spaces.

Respectfully Submitted,

Jim Green, Democrat candidate for Congress, Dist 21, TX, 2000

CHAPTER ELEVEN

WHAT WE NEED TO DO GOING FORWARD IN THE 21ST CENTURY:

Inexplicably "public employment" is seen the same as WPA—where millions are employed directly by the federal government—when that model is not only outmoded—it is insufficient to address our problems in the 21st century.

What we need today is an expanding and contracting public workforce—that expands during downturns in the market, and contracts as employees return to the private sector [Google: The Buffer Stock Employment Model]—triggered anytime our unemployment exceeds "3%" [as "authorized" under Humphrey-Hawkins]-- and least understood: This is an INDISPENSABLE component in the effective functioning of our 21st Century Market.

The market thrives when we have a robust, employed, consuming workforce—our manufacturers are sitting on $2 trillion in cash because they do not have consumers for their products—i.e., absent consumers, they lay off employees—[and the Republican solution, Reaganomics, has acted as an accelerate to this downward spiral—and which Romney promises to return us to if he is elected]!

In short, the above model is a "win-win" solution—the American people win, and capitalism wins!

To achieve this, what is being urged is "The Neighbor-To-Neighbor Job Creation Act": A federally mandated, mutual insurance—owned by our employed [from janitor to CEO] to create a fund to hire/train our unemployed.

To be viable, however, our job creation solution **<u>MUST</u>** contain:

1] Be based on the premise that we have far more work that needs to be done in America, than we have persons to fill these jobs.

2] It MUST have renewable funding.

3] It will not add a dime to our deficit.

To expand briefly, it is currently believed, erroneously, that we need "make work" jobs so that everyone who wants to work will have a job—but this is absurd—and an insult to "Yankee Ingenuity".

We do not have an unemployment crisis from a shortage of jobs, or money—but rather from a shortage of imagination.

Regarding "renewable funding" ALL of our job creation solutions, to date, have been based on the mind-set: "jump start" the market, and the market will in turn create all the jobs we need—and even setting aside that this is untrue, our current job creation is moving at a snail's pace—long past the unemployment benefits drying up—with the CBO projecting that even with the JOBS Act, signed into law on April 6, 2012--it will be 2017 before we return to a barely acceptable 5.5% unemployment rate!

Further, by its nature when we "jump start" --the employment ends when the funding runs out as we learned from the Stimulus—whereas any real fix to our unemployment crisis <u>demands</u> renewable funding....

And whether the electorate will accept an unemployment rate hovering around 8% on election day—is the $64,000 question....

Regarding not adding a dime to our deficit—under The Neighbor-To-Neighbor Job Creation Act [NTN], the <u>funding</u> to reduce our unemployment to 3% comes from an insurance owned by our employed, rather than added to our deficit—

If one is employed in America, participation in this insurance plan is mandatory—similar in concept to our auto insurance or Social Security Insurance [and without question the most successful social program in American history].

Jobs beget jobs--And with a modest policy cost of 4% of salary we can create more "private-sector" jobs in 6 months, that HR 2847, and the JOBS Act, in 6 years— and unlike these laws—NTN will not add a dime to our deficit!

Finally, this is in total concert with the will of the American people, i.e., that "anybody wanting to work should be able to find a job"—and the American people have told our politicians time and again of their willingness to chip in to help their neighbor get a job [and as an <u>insurance</u>, as above, it also protects their continued employment]—it is just that Washington is deaf as an adder!

CHAPTER TWELVE

Hey Mitt Romney….re a Third Party….I'm 82,
but I support the real protest by the American people
in this election—and inexplicably ignored by both of
our major parties….to wit:

According to the FEC, I am a candidate for president
on the Democrat ticket, and specifically urge the
codification of a legal right to work, i.e.: "Work shall
hereafter be the legal right of every citizen, and
Congress shall, except for retirement/disability
programs under federal jurisdiction, make no laws
which will abridge the right of any citizen of legal age,
to work and be a productive citizen."

All of the candidates for president have made
grandiose claims that they will create millions of jobs, if
elected…..and fixing unemployment [hereafter UE] has
been the number one issue in every election in America
since 1975……it is the reason over-flow crowds are
showing up at Trump and Sanders rallies…..to protest
a system that no longer works—with excessive UE 70%
of the time since 1980 [twice that of preceding years]….

**THE LYNCH PIN IN FIXING OUR
UNEMPLOYMENT CRISIS, IS FIXING OUR JOB
CREATION—**

Our tradition for Job Creation since WW II-- and we are chary to admit that our tradition has one foot on the plantation—has been: Cut taxes for the 1%, they will build factories all across our fair land with the windfall of cash, and jobs will rain down like moonbeams—i.e., and in combination with the propaganda that "the market can provide anybody wanting a job, with a job".

Problem is—this method of Job Creation is pure BS, a fairytale—and given automation, alone, is unworkable in a 21st Century market economy----and has resulted in a UE rate below 3% only ONCE since WW II—in 1953—leaving millions jobless in its wake—it has created our inner-cities with 60% minority unemployment—particularly among youth—with drug economies, and an epidemic of gun violence…

The bottom line is: UE is a NO ONE WINS….the jobless lose, civility loses [Ferguson, etc.,], and the Market loses….people do not buy what we manufacture when they are jobless--It is not outsourcing that is stealing our jobs in America---it is our failure to adapt in a changing world….

The solution: HR 1000 [in Committee]; FULL EMPLOYMENT IS A PRO-MARKET CONCEPT, and THE CASE FOR WORK BEING A LEGAL RIGHT, Amazon/Kindle

Jim Green, Democrat opponent to Lamar Smith, 2000

PS This is both tongue-in-cheek, and dead serious….

CHAPTER THIRTEEN

President Obama/Council of Economic Advisers:

Since WW II our method of Job Creation has been based on the propaganda [lie], that "the market can provide anybody wanting a job, with a job"....

And even our "brightest and best", have fallen prey to this erroneous propaganda—BS----for instance, President Carter lost the 1980 election because he failed to grasp the importance of the "legal authorization"—HE SIGNED INTO LAW [15 USC § 3101]--limiting our UE rate to 3%--Carter would have won hands down had he fixed unemployment! And, Democrats—wearing the same blinders, ushered in a House filled with lunatics in the 2010 election—by failing to employ this legal fix to end UE--leaving Washington in paralysis ever since!

Our failure to fix unemployment is the reason over 70% of Americans believe "We are moving in the wrong direction"!

The bottom line is, UNTIL we change the way we create jobs in America—we can forget the slogan by every politician in the 2016 election: "JOBS, JOBS, JOBS"!

The source of this dangerous path is the conservative response to President Truman's FULL EMPLOYMENT BILL OF 1945—to provide employment for our troops returning from WW

II…and the 1% has spent hundreds of millions, since, buying our elections/politicians--to abolish our labor unions, and to instill "at will" employment in EVERY state—only Montana limits "at will" to probationary employees….

But, by being taken in by this BS—Americans have been made to suffer with a method of Job Creation that has not resulted in an unemployment rate below 3% since 1953! Leaving millions jobless in its wake—and in its ineptness has resulted in our inner-cities becoming war zones, with an epidemic of gun violence!

Also, in the interim—from WW II until today—the world economy has undergone enormous socio-economic change—and precipitated by the colliding forces of automation, globalization, technology, etc., reaching critical mass in the mid-1970's—with subsequent "High and persistent unemployment", since….

Further, and as a result of automation, alone, we have had excessive unemployment 70% of the time since 1980 [twice that of preceding years]….

And yet we cling to the archaic and unworkable Job Creation model, above, at the expense of JOBS, and our modern market economy—WHY?

Ref: HR 1000 [in Committee], FULL EMPLOYMENT IS A PRO-MARKET CONCEPT, Amazon

Jim Green, Democrat opponent to Lamar Smith, Congress, 2000

Thank you for contacting the White House!

CHAPTER FOURTEEN

Over the past several decades observing…and often finding what we are doing a puzzlement [such as pretending the 800 Carrier jobs is anything other than a political gimmick—when we need to create 200,000 jobs a month just to keep up with our birthrate] but through the BS, I formulated some solutions to our social problems that I assert will actually work—and being a capitalist, have identified as "Neo-Capitalism". To distinguish from other programs, and to identify, coined the name: ECONOMIC INCLUSIVISM, and have a book on Amazon/Kindle. Since 1996, I have had a web page on the internet: www.Inclusivism.org My thinking has evolved over the years, and have zeroed in on Job Creation—I believe our solution to unemployment to be the most important issue facing America going forward in the 21 Century—but posting, here, are my proposed solutions, defined as Economic Inclusivism:

ECONOMIC INCLUSIVISM: A 21st Century Solution

[Social/Prison Reforms]
1) We need to re-classify all crime in the future as violent or non-violent, and discard the archaic terms felony and misdemeanor. The word felony has been implanted in the public's mind to mean "armed and dangerous", and yet over 70% of our prison inmates (all felons) are in prison for non-violent offenses. As a result, the term "felony" is distracting us from addressing the real problem....the violent offender.

2) We need a much greater use of "Shock" Incarceration (A sentencing alternative I authored in the 1960's); a greater use of fines, restitution, and probation (both civil and criminal), in lieu of incarceration, and fines paid directly to victims instead of the state all as part of an expanded menu of sentencing alternatives. [We have 5% of the world's population, and 25% of all prison inmates on earth, in our prisons! If we had the same proportion of inmates to general population as the rest of the civilized world, we would have 400,000 persons incarcerated, not 2,200,000, as we do at present! And yet our PR is that we are the most free country in the world? We daily turn non-violent persons into violent career criminals, with over 99% released back into society, making life in America MORE dangerous, not less! And the grizzly stabbing death, in Illinois, of 8 and 9 year old girls, on Mother's Day, 2005, by a recently released inmate, is a textbook example of this inept approach.....when on earth are we going to accept that to whatever degree....we are also part of the problem? Prison should be a last resort, not first!] We can correct this by mandating that our legislatures return to the pre-1988 (pre the Willie Horton ad) standard: For every $1 budgeted for prisons, $5 MUST be budgeted for the education of our children. This appx ratio was not set by statute, but rather by tradition and common sense. At present, we budget more for prisons than educating our youth, and were not becoming a police state?

3) We need to create Federal Regional Diagnostic and Treatment Centers, for the diagnosis and treatment of the violent offender. We have learned a great deal

about violent behavior in recent years (see www.brainplace.com), and yet we do not have a cohesive or concerted national program or policy in America for dealing with this national epidemic and disgrace. The sheer numbers of homicides by handguns, alone, tells the whole story: Canada 151, Australia 57, Germany 373, Japan 19, England and Wales 54, the United States 11,789! When we add in all deaths by guns, including the fact that 9 children are killed by guns everyday in America, our gun violence escalates to a staggering 28,663! Also, we need to allow for voluntary admissions to these Centers, to prevent juvenile and family violence. It is essential that we seek out "problem-solving", not "punishment" oriented solutions, which actually exacerbate crime.

4) We need to pick-up the lead taken by England, in treating drug addiction as a "medical" rather than a "criminal" problem, so that we can EFFECTIVELY curb drug-related crime, and keep drugs out of the hands of our youth. To demonstrate how specious our thinking has become in this area, alcohol and tobacco kill ten of thousands of persons annually, and yet these drugs are not classified as "dangerous". The tiny handful of persons with "addictive personalities" has totally shaped our drug policies while "addiction", in all of its forms, can only EFFECTIVELY be treated with a medical solution. We have wasted billions on interdiction, and yet, youth drug abuse is actually increasing.

[Economic Reforms]
5) To address our insidious practice of "exclusion",

Congress must enforce a citizen's legal right to work (1), as enacted by Congress in "The Full Employment Act of 1946", and as outlined in the Democratic National Platform position asserting "Opportunity to every American". The right to work and be a productive member of one's society is also a human right. Accordingly, we must ratify the following constitutional amendment: "Work shall hereafter be the legal right of every citizen, and Congress shall, except for retirement/disability programs under federal jurisdiction, make no laws which will abridge the right of any citizen of legal age, to work and be a productive citizen." [Our lapse in enlightenment regarding this urgently needed systemic change -- believed by the ignorant and uninformed to be "communism" -- combined with some really peculiar notions about guns, is the cause for almost all violent crime in America. This is a "practical" rather than a "liberal" solution in our 21st Century economy, a point totally lost on ideologues. This is not a "safety net" (the conservative propaganda buzz term to undermine "social" programs), this is recognizing within each of us a "human right". The distinction is as different as night and day. Further, rather than being a wildly radical idea, a recent Zogby poll found that "86% of Americans think the government should provide a job to anyone who wants one", according to the April 4, 2005 issue of The Nation. Economic Inclusivism, however, does not ask that the government provide a job, but rather recognizes within each citizen the legal right to work and be a prouctive member of the society, as a HUMAN RIGHT. Also, For clarity, I am a capitalist. I support limited interference on the part of government in the free enterprise system, and find the ownership of "business", or a government controlled economy, as currently incorporated in both socialism and communism, to be patently absurd. We will always have government controls so that we have safe food, and medicine, etc., and we rightfully should have, that is separate and apart from the government doing, what a free enterprise business can do better. I would vehemently disagree that our recognition within each citizen a "human right" to work and be a productive citizen to be an interference with the free enterprise system, and it would have more of a psychological impact on the individual, than an economic impact on the economy, as it currently exists. A person wishing to become a doctor, will still become a doctor, or a CEO, or bartender, whatever…..people do what is most compatible with their nature and talents and Economic Inclusuvism would not change that. Indeed, it in some cases it would provide a greater assist in their reaching their goal, than is currently available, and it is much more efficient in utilizing our greatest resource: humans, that our current system. Most importantly, it is the right thing to do].

6) To ensure enforcement/fund this legal right, Congress would create a privately owned, federally mandated, mutual insurance plan, with limited ownership by each person who works, which would provide work/training to any citizen who applies. Work could include: Child care for low income working families, building a high-speed rail system, the urgent need outlined by the NEA for School Modernization, the creation of Federal Regional Diagnostic and

Treatment Centers for the diagnosis and treatment of the violent offender [HINT: convert our excessive new prisons into said Centers], repairing our rotting infrastructure (the list of social benefits is endless). As owners of this plan, each worker would vote on proposed national projects and dividends would be paid annually from unused funds. A projected cost of 8% would be less than the worker currently pays for welfare. [Like Social Security and military retirement moneys, Economic Inclusivism would STRENGTHEN, not weaken the business community....these steps are necessary to preserve, not harm capitalism in a rapidly changing economy...Bill Gates became the richest man in the world because of these monies percolating through the economy....If W (and the wacko Neo-Con ideas) was the president in the 30's, instead of FDR, Bill Gates would be on the street with a "Will work for food" signs.....and further this will prevent our further movement down the erroneous path towards communism or towards the other extreme, fascism (our current movement), both of which require a dictator, and the wholesale loss of our civil liberties, to hold the government in place.]

7) Since this program of "inclusion" would address 95% of our social ills (crime, welfare, drugs, etc., and exacerbated in many cases by inept Band-Aid programs), the federal budget could be greatly reduced and our current Federal Income Tax would be replaced with a National Sales Tax, value-added tax, a national lottery, or some combination of taxes other than our current Federal Income Tax. We currently spend 26 billion annually for the Internal Revenue Service, and

corporations and individuals spend trillions trying to get around the Tax Code, all of which is passed on to us, the consumer, in the higher cost of consumer goods.

7a)A Universal Healtcare System is an essential ingredient of a sane society!

CHAPTER FIFTEEN

President Obama/Presidential Innovation Fellows/Council of Economic Advisers/First Lady:

Both Democrats and Republicans have proclaimed that this election is about "Jobs, Jobs, Jobs" [a direct quote by Trump]—but the reality is that we are at the same juncture in our social/economic evolution—regarding Job Creation—as when us humans believed that world travel was out of the question, because consensus had it that the world is flat.....

For instance, it is universally believed, today, that "the market can provide anybody wanting a job, with a job"—and even our "brightest and best" appear incapable of thinking of Job Creation, except via this prism....

And Exhibit One is HR 2847—the major legislation to address unemployment [hereafter UE], following the Great Crash in 2008....

Officially tagged as the HIRE Act—it is "stop-gap" [rather than Job Creation] legislation--the same as EVERY like act since 1980—in theory, to bridge us over until the market creates all the jobs we need.....combined with magical thinking and the flat world belief that the market could actually do this—as our economy has limped along on a flat tire...

And, when even a casual look at the data reveals that this scheme is absurd—i.e., the above "belief"--that has

SOLELY driven our Job Creation since WW II—has not resulted in a UE rate below 3% since 1953! In a few words, the path we are on **DOESN'T WORK**—and is more at home on a Santa Claus wish list, than problem solving!

And it has left millions jobless in its wake, and has resulted in our inner-cities becoming war zones, with drug economies, and an epidemic of gun violence!

It appears that the mind automatically defaults to ideology as a means to justify staying on a path—year after year—**THAT DOESN'T WORK**—with words like "capitalism-good", "communism-bad"—when neither is relevant, and common sense, alone, tells us that the mechanic cannot fix the engine, without the proper tools….

In short, we need look no further than Flint to understand the devastating results of UE—and yet we stood on one foot and then the other in our "wing and a prayer" scheme—as Flint, as well as the rest of the Rust Belt rotted into decay…..

We need to change course—because the path we are on **DOESN'T WORK**—and the result is unconscionable…..

Re: HR 1000 [in Committee], **FULL EMPLOYMENT IS A PRO-MARKET CONCEPT, and THE NEIGHBOR-TO-NEIGHBOR JOB CREATION ACT,** Amazon/Kindle

Jim Green, Democrat opponent to Lamar Smith, TX, Congress 2000

CHAPTER SIXTEEN

Posted on President-elect Trump's website

A German-national informed regarding a long-perplexing question: Why, on God's earth, did the German people fall prey to a monster like Hitler? To which he instantly replied "Because he put them to work"---and with over 70% of Americans asserting we are "moving in the wrong direction", the importance of Full Employment in America is indisputable! To borrow from "Chitty, Chitty…."—We Democrats had the "legal authorization", on the books in 2009---to reduce our UE to "3%"—permanently--but "we muffed it"—and in 2010, a retaliatory electorate filled the House with lunatics, and left Washington in paralysis ever since! Will the Trump presidency recognize, where we Democrats failed---and given "automation", alone, going forward--that our ONLY PATH to create the "millions of jobs" promised, is via the "legal authorization" in Public Law 15 USC § 3101—and enforced via deficit-neutral, Pro-Market HR 1000 [in Committee], or like solution--THE NEIGHBOR-TO-NEIGHBOR JOB CREATION ACT, Amazon? Trump is not beholden to persons who don't know their arse from a hole in the ground—[like President Obama's Job Creation advisers in 2009, and/or will suggest corrupt and unworkable Supply Side]--and Trump has an excellent opportunity to do the right thing on behalf of the millions who voted for him—AND VOTED FOR CHANGE! Time will tell…….Job Creation can easily get lost in ideology—and incompetence takes over—the solution to Job

Creation is based on "what works, and what doesn't"—
and getting lost in ideology is absurd! And evidenced
by the fact that what we have been doing since WW II
doesn't work in our 21st Century market economy!
Indeed, given "automation", alone, Humphrey-
Hawkins is INDISPENSABLE to the EFFECTIVE
functioning of our 21st Century market economy! Jim
Green, Democrat candidate for Congress, TX, 2000

Thank You For Your Support

CHAPTER SEVENTEEN

President Obama/Council of Economic Advisers:

The most important lesson to be learned from our sluggish recovery is that the world has changed, and to keep pace it is imperative that we change how we create jobs.

Historically, every recession since WW II has been followed by a strong recovery--and every credible economic experts agrees that our inability, today, to create jobs [our high unemployment] has been central in our resulting sluggish recovery—

And the impact on the elderly has been the most evident, and one of the hardest hit....

In 2010, and for the first time since 1975 when the Cost of Living Adjustment [COLA] rate was created by law, to protect our elderly and disabled from pernicious inflation—the COLA in 2010 was "0.0"—

There was a COLA adjustment in EVERY previous year....but it didn't stop there and COLA was again flat-lined at "0.0" in 2011, and again in 2016-—while in the same time frame we had a cumulative 12.7% increase in inflation in the same almost 8 years.

And while we can all celebrate the turnaround after the Republicans trashed our economy in 2008--it is evident by COLA, alone, that we have been in an extremely anemic recovery—

The bottom line, however, is the correlation between: "High Unemployment & Sluggish Recovery/Economy" —the former causing the latter.

Since WW II, and the [FULL] EMPLOYMENT ACT OF 1946 [to create jobs for our returning troops], we have had two distinct paths to Job Creation in America:

1] The belief/propaganda [lie] that the market can create all the jobs we need, and….

2] Outlined in pro-market, deficit-neutral Humphrey-Hawkins [hereafter HH] in 1978—that would trigger Job Creation from a "reservoir of public employees" anytime our UE rate rises above "3%"…..[currently HR 1000, in Committee].

The plutocracy/oligarchy hated [didn't understand] HH, however, and with hundreds of millions to buy our elections Washington pretty much hated HH too…..i.e., its "legal authorization" has never been enforced….

And evident by our current recovery—with President Obama ill-advised by his Council of Economic Advisers—i.e., given "automation" alone, eliminating jobs it is evident we are long over-due in changing course—we are long over-due in enforcing the "legal authorization" in HH.

Ref: FULL EMPLOYMNET IS A PRO-MARKET CONCEPT, Amazon/Kindle

Jim Green, Democrat opponent to Lamar Smith, Congress, 2000

CHAPTER EIGHTEEN

The following is a letter from U.S. Representative John Conyers, posted on the internet, re his law--H.R. 1000, the "Humphrey-Hawkins Full Employment and Training Act"

"Since 2000 more than 50,000 manufacturing facilities in the U.S. have closed and roughly 50,000 industrial jobs have been lost each month. Now service sector jobs, where the remaining two-thirds of all workers are currently employed, are disappearing. Because of, but not limited to technology advances, these middle-income jobs are not likely to come back, effectively hollowing out the America's middle class and leaving millions of unemployed and underemployed workers with limited future prospects. The effect of these trends on American jobs were significantly aggravated by the "Great Recession."

"Meanwhile, in spite of the Great Recession, the wealthiest 1% of Americans has become even richer. The share of income taken by the top 1% has more than doubled by 2007, U.S. corporations became flush with record profits, and the stock market has rebounded to all-time highs. All while stagnate wages for the working poor and middle-class remained and, in some cases declined, over the same time period.

"During the Great Depression, President Roosevelt's New Deal put millions of Americans back to work building roads, dams, bridges, parks and electrification systems.

"There is no reason why America cannot have a 21st century "New Deal," where unemployed Americans can be gainfully employed rebuilding our crumbling infrastructure and strengthening our communities.

It is my hope that with the reintroduction of my bill, the "Humphrey-Hawkins Full Employment and Training Act," Congress will begin to seriously examine the idea that the federal government can, and must, play a major role in putting Americans back to work. H.R. 1000 is deficit neutral, because it is paid for by a modest tax on stock and bond transactions by Wall Street trading firms. Having already received a significant bailout by American taxpayers, it is only fair that Wall Street pay Main Street back by helping put America back to work."

Sincerely,
John Conyers, Jr.

CHAPTER NINETEEN

Letter to the editor:

Will politics never change?

A Republican candidate for president said "On next January 20, there will begin in Washington, the biggest unraveling, unsnarling, untangling operation in our nation's history."

But before Republican ideologues say "right on" regarding their belief in unraveling President Obama's administration— this was from a speech by Republican candidate Tom Dewey, and directed at President Truman, in 1948!

Given the political rhetoric you would think President Truman [and President Obama] couldn't even tie their own shoes— albeit, President Truman had ended WWII [while President Obama has rescued America from another Great Depression, and got bin Laden, etc., etc.,].

And other parallels between these two elections are even more striking. For instance, Truman was outraged by what he called a "Do nothing Congress"— and he went on to warn the electorate that "The country cannot afford another Republican Congress." No informed American will dispute that, today….

The most startling parallel, however, is when Truman said of the Republican Congress on a stump speech "It is a sad tale of the sell out of the American people to these gluttons of privilege— these cold men who skim the cream from our natural resources to satisfy their own greed."

This could have been said yesterday, and yet, it was said by President Truman 68 years ago!

Finally, President Truman offered some words of wisdom to the American electorate on the danger of returning our government back to the Republicans [as true today, as then] "I'm just waking you up to the fact that this is YOUR fight— and YOU are going to be the loser [if you return the White House back to the Republicans]."

And, as every student of History knows, and in spite of the inexcusable headline error by the Chicago Tribune "DEWEY DEFEATS TRUMAN"— President Truman did win—and kept the White House where it belongs— with a Democrat!

Ref: IT IS IMPOSSIBLE TO BE A CHRISTIAN, AND VOTE REPUBLICAN, Amazon/Kindle

Jim Green, Democrat opponent to Lamar Smith, Congress, 2000

Bio: http://www.amazon.com/James-L.-Jim-Green/e/B001KHZIMM/ref=ntt_dp_epwbk_0

CHAPTER TWENTY

President Obama/Council of Economic Advisers:

THE OUTRAGE BY BERNIE/DONALD FOLLOWERS?

While we celebrate 255,000 jobs, and a steady 4.9%--in the 8/5/16 Jobs Report—the fact is---the oligarchy/folks running the show in America JUST-DON'T-GET-IT……

We could attribute to "Old habits are hard to break"…..and while this cannot be cited as the sole reason—it is a factor---in the oligarchy/Washington's inability to bring our Job Creation in America into the 21st Century….particularly given "automation", alone….

What they "don't get" is that Since WW II our Job Creation in America has been driven by a single premise [propaganda/lie]: "The market can provide anybody wanting a job, with a job"—problem is, it is PURE BS!

And evident by the fact that this Job Creation model has not resulted in an unemployment [hereafter UE] rate below 3% since 1953—and in the interim has created our inner-cities--with 60% minority UE, drug economies, and an epidemic of gun violence!

And there is something quite disturbing when Washington stood on one foot and then the other, and

via magical thinking, let Flint, and the rest of the Rust Belt rot into decay—the "magical thinking" was the belief that "No problem"--the market will fix this—particularly when it was OBVIOUS BY THE RESULT, that the market is INCAPABLE of fixing this problem!

An indifference, incidentally, that was infinitely magnified by the fact that since 1978--Washington has had the "legal authorization" to restrict our UE rate in America to "3%"—PERMANENTLY-- [Pro-Market 15 USC § 3101—and currently HR 1000—in Committee]—laws that are INDISPENSABLE to the EFFECTIVE functioning of our 21st Century MARKET ECONOMY!

Unemployment is a NO ONE WINS proposition…..the jobless lose, civility loses [Ferguson, etc.,], and the market loses, to wit:

THE LAW OF DIMINISHED INCOME TO THE MARKET FROM UNEMPLOYMENT [hereafter D/UE LAW]

Short Definition:

3% is the zero-sum threshold above which unemployment starts substantially undermining the Market--and the loss in income to the Market is compounded exponentially with each percentage point of increase in unemployment, above 3%.

Ref: FULL EMPLOYMENT IS A PRO-MARKET CONCEPT; FIX UNEMPLOYMENT, AND THIS WILL FIX THE MARKET; and THE NEIGHBOR-TO-NEIGHBOR JOB CREATION ACT, Amazon/Kindle

Jim Green, Democrat opponent to Lamar Smith, 2000

PS: Apologize for CAPS—your software does not provide emphasis

Thank you for contacting the White House!

CHAPTER TWENTY-ONE

President Obama/Council of Economic Advisers:

Two-thirds of the world's 7 billion population live in market-driven economies—1.2 billion are in the OECD, with China and India, alone, adding an additional 2.6 billion, and anyone who doesn't think China is a market economy, hasn't shopped at Wal-Mart….

The over-arching point, here, is the unwritten, but nevertheless pervasive/pernicious belief in our market-driven economies is that "the market can provide anybody wanting a job, with a job"….it is pernicious because it causes the "rank and file" to oppose climate change—in their belief that this is their ONLY means to get a Job! And, when, in fact, it is BS, NOT supported by the data or empirical evidence….

With the result that our record in job creation is deplorable—i.e., this methodology is woefully inadequate, as we inch along, and 5 years after the declared end of the Great Recession—we still have almost 10 million jobless Americans….

The question NOT being asked in Washington is: How do we address our pernicious unemployment in America—when the market cannot create enough jobs?

Had we put a lawnmower engine in the Saturn V rocket, on our Apollo 11 trip to the moon—we would never have gotten there…a perfect metaphor for our current method of job creation in America—which leaves millions jobless for years—and skewed against minorities…..

The fact is, ONLY ONCE in the past 65 years—under our "market only job creation" model—has our unemployment rate dropped below "3%"—in 1953—and in spite of the "legal authorization" in the U.S., since 1978, to limit our unemployment to 3% [15 USC § 3101].

In short, at NO time since 1978, and to this day, should our unemployment rate in America exceed 3% [HR 1000]---when, in fact, our jobless rate, today, is double that—and it will be 2017 before we return to even an anemic 5.5%, as projected by the CBO--

And the irony is that unemployment is a "NO ONE WINS" proposition—both the jobless lose, and the market loses, to wit:

> 3% is the zero-sum threshold above which unemployment starts substantially undermining the Market--and the loss in income to the Market is compounded exponentially with each percentage point of increase in unemployment, above 3%.

FULL EMPLOYMENT IS A PRO-MARKET CONCEPT [Amazon]

Jim Green, Democrat opponent to Lamar Smith, Congress, 2000

CHAPTER TWENTY-TWO

President Obama/Council of Economic Advisers:

A German-national advised—in response to a question perplexing me for years—"Why on earth did the German people, with their rich cultural history, fall under the spell of a monster like Hitler"? And without a moments hesitation he said "Because he put them to work".

There is a message in there of vital importance: The value humans place on being a productive member of society—the value we place on "work"—even raising the question if it should become a Human Right?

And while giving lip service to the plight of the unemployed--our market economies, the OECD, which includes the U.S., all suffer from high unemployment—and none address unemployment as a "social" problem—with serious social consequences--WE, as a society have the RESPONSIBILITY to address—Rather they leave the creation of employment up to the whims of the market--And if the market fails, the unemployed are out of luck!

Which raises the question: The market suffers when people are unemployed—and the unemployed suffer when they are not working—so WHY on earth do our market-driven economies continue down such an unrewarding--a lose-lose path—where the market loses, and the unemployed lose?

The late Peter Drucker advocated for CEO salaries being limited to 20 times that of the lowest paid employee [the Swiss recently had on the ballot 12 times]—but it is argued that a brain-drain would occur if we didn't leave this to the market to set CEO salaries—

And whether or not this is true—WHY on earth do we persist in the anachronistic BELIEF that the market can provide anybody wanting a job, with a job [untrue since the mid-1970's]--particularly, and given automation, alone--an expanding and contracting public workforce is an INDISPENSABLE component to the EFFECTIVE functioning of a modern market economy?

Indeed, in the U.S. we have the "legal authority" on the books [15 USC § 3101], to limit our unemployment to 3%--in short, at no time should our unemployment exceed 3%--So why does Washington avoid this legal authority as if it were the plague—such as indifference to deficit—neutral solutions, i.e., HR 870, or via Social Insurance in The Neighbor-To-Neighbor Job Creation Act?

Please see: WHY WE CAN'T FIX UNEMPLOYMENT, Amazon

Highest regards,

Jim Green, Democrat opponent to Lamar Smith, Congress, 2000

CHAPTER TWENTY-THREE

President Obama/Council of Economic Advisers:

Capitalism is ideal in producing and selling corn flakes and cars—It doesn't work in solving "social problems" such as unemployment and our healthcare....

And when we have tried "privatization" to solve our social problems—it has been a disaster:

Essential programs have been cut—such as the elimination of text books from the Job Corps education program—to increase profits, and cronyism has run rampant—

And in our "for profit" healthcare system, billions of dollars are siphoned away from the premiums we send in—and do not go to the healthcare of ANYONE—but rather is used to pay for lobbyists, to make the CEO's filthy rich—and spent on propaganda ads to keep it that way!

Further, it attracts a few who see healthcare as a means to get rich, rather than cure the ill....

The truth is, we currently have a blended system—and they are, in fact, indispensable to each other:

Were it not for Social Security Insurance moneys percolating up through our economy in 2008—we would not be talking about having narrowly averted another Great Depression—We would be buried in one!

Social Insurance is a vital ingredient in building a vibrant and decent society—And, invent a better widget, sell the company for a million bucks, and retire in South Florida [capitalism]—is as well a vital ingredient in building a vibrant and decent society.

So why do we have this war of words pitting the two against each other—rather than educating the American people regarding the indispensable symbiotic relationship they have to each other?

Were it not for the $2 trillion + Washington infuses into the economy annually—capitalism would fold in a NY Second!

And yet, most Republicans ask God in their prayers at night to be protected from becoming communists, or socialists, or even worse "liberals"—i.e., ignorant of what the terms mean…..

And this war of words disguises that the Republican Party, today, is not the Pro-Market party they boast—

but rather their policies are, in fact, Anti-Market—
destructive to capitalism!

Pandering to the GREED of their wealthiest
contributors—the Republican One and Only
program—is NOT a Pro-Market concept!

Another misnomer in the war of words, is right-wing
invented "entitlement"—a word that should be banned
from honest discussion—do we refer to our auto
insurance as an "entitlement"?

And when Social Security Insurance brings in more
that it pays out, i.e., is deficit-neutral--how is that an
"entitlement", and why is it portrayed in our graphs as
a "government expense"—or even included in these
graphs? If a corporation reported a massive loss on a
product they in fact made money—they would be
charged with fraud in a New York Minute!

The list goes on—please see: OUR GREED AND
IGNORANCE, on Amazon/Kindle

Jim Green, Democrat congressional opponent to
Lamar Smith, 2000

CHAPTER TWENTY-FOUR

President Obama/Council of Economic Advisers:

THE HISTORY OF HUMPHREY-HAWKINS

The historic March On Washington, and Dr. King's "I had a dream" speech, in 1963, was a march for JOBS.

At that time, and to this day, our job creation in America has been based on the premise that "the market can provide anybody wanting a job, with a job—

And yet, only ONCE since WW II has this method of job creation resulted in an unemployment rate below 3%--in 1953—leaving millions jobless in its wake.

Following Dr. Kings death in 1968, civil rights leaders, including Jesse Jackson, annually marched on Dr. King's birthday for legislation that would address our pervasive unemployment in America.

Their demand was not without legal foundation. In 1946, President Truman signed into law the [FULL] EMPLOYMENT ACT OF 1946, to provide employment for our troops returning from WW II.

The 1%, however, balked at American employees having rights—particularly a right to employment [the model which exists to this day]—and the law was never implemented.

Ironically, Australia enacted a law similar to President Truman's Employment Act—and for the same reason—and for the next 30 years [and until the ill-winds of neo-liberalism in the mid-1970's] Australia's employment model was based on the premise that "anybody wanting to work should be able to find a job"—with 2% or less unemployment common. Australians still refer to this as their "Golden Age".

As a result of the demand by civil rights leaders for legislation, however, in 1978 President Carter signed into law—what is commonly known as the Humphrey-Hawkins Full Employment Act [15 USC § 3101].

The law provides the "legal authorization" for the creation of a "reservoir of public employees" anytime our unemployment in America exceeds "3%". That is, and to this day—at no time should our unemployment rate in America exceed 3%.

The money in politics, however, has prevented this law from being implemented!

Notwithstanding, a lone Congressman, Conyers [and a growing number of co-sponsors] has diligently worked to implement Humphrey-Hawkins [currently, deficit-neutral HR 1000, in Committee].

And, singularly, unemployment is the most pernicious problem facing America, today....

Ref: FULL EMPLOYMENT IS A PRO-MARKET CONCEPT, Amazon

Jim Green, Democrat opponent to Lamar Smith, 2000

Thank You!
Thank you for contacting the White House.

CHAPTER TWENTY-FIVE

President Obama:

It is impossible to reform our broken criminal justice system—absent our creating a viable job creation program in America.

And while it is generally believed that we do have a job creation program, in fact, we do not!

We have the BELIEF that "the market can provide anybody wanting a job, with a job"—but the data shows that only ONCE since WW II has this belief resulted in an unemployment rate below 3%--in 1953— leaving millions jobless in its wake-- and has resulted in:

60% minority unemployment in our inner-cities, with drug economies, and an epidemic of homicides [i.e., not fixing unemployment has turned our inner-cities into war zones, and created a breeding ground for our inexplicable incarceration rate].

Further this "belief" has been a stumbling block in finding a solution for our pervasive unemployment--In short, we have not been looking for a solution—because our policy makers believe we have one—and apparently few have looked at the data....

Also, ignored in the discussion is that unemployment is a "social" problem, with adverse, and oft severe social

consequences—both for the individual, as well as the larger society [i.e., it is the responsibility of the larger society to solve]—

With tentacles integral to all of the social problems facing Americans, today—for instance, ending unemployment is integral to Criminal Justice Reform, and the repair of our crumbling infrastructure….

Further, in 1975 we spent $5 educating our youth, for every $1 we spent on prisons…..by the mid-1990's [with the American people having been terrorized by the Willie Horton ad—and on an hysterical prison building spree] our competing tax dollars tipped in favor of prisons—and at present we spend more on prisons, than on educating our youth.

The irony in all of this is that we have the "legal authorization", on the books to reduce our unemployment rate to 3%, tomorrow [15 USC § 3101—and deficit-neutral HR 1000, currently in Committee]—and also ignored in this context, is that President Obama had a weapon in addressing our economic meltdown in 2008, not available to FDR— and that is the $800 billion in Social Security Insurance claims percolating up through our economy—and in the absence of which--We would be buried in another Great Depression!

Turning the page—and given "automation", alone, is critical going forward in the 21st Century—and is a "win-win"—the American people win, and the market wins….

Ref: FULL EMPLOYMENT IS A PRO-MARKET CONCEPT, Amazon

Jim Green, Democrat opponent to Lamar Smith, 2000

CHAPTER TWENTY-SIX

I didn't write the following. It is a cut and paste from FACEBOOK, or some blog [would like to give credit if knew the author]--but it is so on target regarding how "fear" is driving Conservative policy in America today—i.e., is undermining America and our progress—and relegating America to a Third World country status, rather than a world leader—FDR had it on the nose in "All we have to fear, is fear itself"…at his inaugural in 1933….

"Conservatives are such cowards: they are afraid of gay people getting married or serving in the military; they are afraid of bringing terrorists to super max prisons in the US from which no one has ever escaped; they are afraid of the boy scouts letting gay kids in; they are afraid of everyone voting and are constantly suppressing the vote under some bogus voter fraud theory; they are afraid of letting students vote at their universities; they are afraid of women having the right to choose; they even are afraid of women getting contraception [the real issue actually is a women's agency and control over their bodies]; they are afraid of immigration reform leading to citizenship because they are afraid of-- name whatever reason; they are afraid of mandating gun purchasers to undergo background checks for crazy people and terrorists; they are afraid of people smoking pot; they are afraid of climate change being real and contradicting their beloved Bible; they are afraid of legitimate campaign reform; they are afraid of Muslims; they are afraid of blacks; they are afraid of atheists; they are afraid of hippies; they are afraid of socialists; they are probably still afraid of monsters under their beds; they are just rank cowards and keep making things up to be afraid of."

CHAPTER TWENTY-SEVEN

[I couldn't resist including this...and yes I am the author.....]

A MESSAGE FROM GOD

MANY CENTURIES AGO, a man of the cloth, we don't know his name, and in a flash of insight (perhaps induced by peyote) told his flock that "sex is a sin". And lo and behold he learned that by taking a very natural and healthy part of our life and turning it into something that was "dirty and nasty", that he could imprison his flock, and fill his coffers, and hallelujah it was a great day for the Lord!

Quickly, his miracle spread to other churches in his village, and then to the next village, and then the next county, and then state, and soon it spread to all the churches in the ancient world, and all of their flocks cowed in fear and shame and became imprisoned, and their coffers over-floweth. Hallelujah, it was a great day for the Lord!

And to keep the myth alive they started inventing stories, half-baked stories, that made no sense to anyone who is rational, such as "Mary was a virgin"— well, she just had to be a virgin because she would never partake in anything that was dirty and nasty, like sex (if you're doing it right), and this was necessary to make "sex is a sin" make sense...so they invented a Mary that was "sinless"--you get the picture. And their coffers over-floweth. Hallelujah, it was a great day for the Lord!

No one seemed to be bothered that when we play tricks on the human mind by taking something that is very natural and healthy, such as sex, and make it dirty and nasty that all kinds of bad things happen to the human mind:

Such as most pedophiles, and most serial killers, and voting Republican, and unwarranted suicides, and most mental illness, and unwanted pregnancies. (Teens not wanting to have sex is the perversion, not the other way around, and by replacing sex education and condoms, with unrealistic "abstinence", and by using blather about "low self-esteem" to shame them into not "sinning"—We have a teen pregnancy in the U.S. twice that of England and Canada!).

But none of this mattered, because their coffers over-floweth, and Hallelujah, it is a great day for the Lord!

There is a cure--------Tell our right-wing hypocrites, who Judge, rather than "Judge not".... to shove it....

GOD

ABOUT THE AUTHOR: I was employed in our Criminal Justice System for a cumulative 20 years as a probation officer, with 5 of those years as a chief probation officer. I authored the concept of "Shock Incarceration" which became law in Kansas in 1970, and then was adopted in numerous jurisdictions in the U.S. and also spread to Europe—it is currently identified in the U.S. as "Boot Camp" [as the means to "shock" the young offender—and a total distortion of my original intent—like many ideas, once released, they take on a life of their own]. I also instigated establishment of the first Court Psychiatric Clinic in the U.S., in conjunction with psychiatrists from the Menninger Foundation, as a chief probation officer. Finally, I was the Democrat candidate for Congress, District 21, TX, 2000. I would most define myself as a Social Ecologist-- [albeit my degree is in Psychology]. My web page is www.Inclusivism.org –which has been on the internet since 1996.
http://www.amazon.com/James-L.-Jim-Green/e/B001KHZIMM/ref=ntt_dp_epwbk_0

A BRIEF ADDENDUM: When the U.S. Supreme Court denied certiorari—where the violation of my constitutional rights were obvious, and criminal negligence on the part of the government defendants in the death of our son, equally obvious—[detailed in THE HARVARD BOYS CLUB, Amazon/Kindle]--I filed a Petition for Rehearing [which is automatic]— and included the following. The Clerk of the U.S. Supreme Court called me at my work in California, and asked that I withdraw the "cartoon" [a reprint from The NEW YORKER] from my Petition. I refused on the basis of the First Amendment, and it remains in the archives at the U.S. Supreme Court [Docket #: 79-1627], to this day. The wording [not that clear] is: "Excellent, excellent. A fine blend of truths, half-truths, and blatant falsehoods".

"Excellent, excellent. A fine blend of truths, half-truths,
and blatant falsehoods."

PARTIAL LIST: BOOKS BY THIS AUTHOR ON AMAZON/KINDLE/BN:

•**THE HARVARD BOYS CLUB: Hitler's Assault On Our Freedoms From His Grave**

•**MY LETTERS TO PRESIDENT OBAMA: Confessions Of A Compulsive Letter Writer**

•**OUR GREED AND IGNORANCE: Poses A Far Greater Threat To America, Than Terrorism**

•**LETTERS ON STEROIDS: Confessions Of A Compulsive Letter-To-The-Editor Writer**

•**THE FIRST TIME I HAD SEX: And, The Religious Intolerance Attack On America**

•**WHY PRESIDENT OBAMA LOST THE 2012 ELECTION: A Wake-Up Call**

•**ECONOMIC INCLUSIVISM: Neo-Capitalism/An Anthology: Inclusive pro-market solutions to our social problems**

•**AMERICA IS ONE SICK MF: Why Greed-Driven America Went Off The Rails….**

•**EVERY GIVEN SUNDAY: A Scientific Formula To Predict NFL Games**

And others….http://www.amazon.com/James-L.-Jim-Green/e/B001KHZIMM/ref=ntt_dp_epwbk_0